I0622906

TABLE OF CONTENTS

NICOLETTE A. EASLY

Chapter 1

THE JOSEPHS

*W*ell, it's Sunday again in the Joseph household, my favorite day of the week. Like every Sunday morning and any morning, I was lying in bed listening to the sounds of my daddy's voice travel through the apartment. This was the norm in our household. He was our third alarm clock after my mom would yell continuously, "Ya'll better get up for church," at least four or five times.

"Emmanuel, Narah, Elijah, and Ezekiel," my daddy yelled. "Get up. Do not make me late for church this morning!" That phrase was said every Sunday by my daddy. It never failed. He was getting closer and closer to my bedroom door. I was just hoping he would pass me by, knowing good and well that was not happening. See, the thing is, once again, I stayed up all Saturday night, knowing what Sunday morning would bring. I did my usual - I stayed up late watching *Martin* and *Fresh Prince* reruns and *Street Flavor* with my brothers. Look, *Martin* was something serious to me. If anyone canceled plans with me, that was cool because I would definitely lay in bed and watch *Martin*. I still go to sleep with it playing in the background till this day; it's like my melatonin.

We would be awakened at eight o'clock in the morning. *Bang! Bang! Bang!* At my door, "Narah, get up, or I will leave you. You are always the last one out this door." I smiled under my covers, hoping for the best, thinking that if I played sleep long enough, eventually I would get left. I could smell my mom ironing last-minute shirts, pants, and ties. Anything we did not get out on Saturday night was done before we walked out the door for church. My dad, Mr. David Matthews Joseph, was a preacher and soon-to-be pastor of our home church.

It was the five of us every Sunday, my brothers and I, and my daddy. My mama chose not to go for her own reasons, which we all understood even though she never really came out and told us until we got older. We never really hounded her about it because, no matter what, she was still our mom and first lady of our church, whether it was acknowledged or not. I often felt like she was ignored because she wasn't there by my dad's side in the traditional way. I wasn't looking for anyone to praise her but just acknowledge her. When she was much younger, she felt a sense of judgment. She wouldn't wear those long dresses that hid her ankles. I mean, she just wasn't that girl! She wore just a hint of makeup. She was this little woman with curves who dressed more modern yet still very classy and respectable for church. But some people looked at her like she was committing a crime.

There were other things that kept her from church. Mind you; I said church, not God. Let us just keep that in mind, people. It's great to go to church to hear the word and fellowship with others. I love church, but what if that building were not there? Would you just not worship God? Or not believe in him? Of course not. Look, church hurt is a real thing. Back in those days, though, I do not think they really had a name for it like they do today, but it is a real thing. Church hurt is basically when you are led to believe the people you fellowship with are rooting for you and praying for you, but instead, they are judging you, they turn up their noses at you, and they talk about you behind your back. The people who are supposed to serve the same God as you are doing you dirty. So you end up leaving the church because now your presumption of church is all the same. That type of hurt can turn someone away. My mama always said that just because they are sitting in church does not make them saved. You do have fake church people, unfortunately. That's why you have to have God within you daily.

We would always get to church a little late, and, of course, I was to blame. I was the slowest out of the house, into and out of the car. Being late was my forte. Look, I was not happy about it. I was always the last and slowest to get ready, but of course, that was not my daddy's forte. Being on time was important to him. He had to be there to open up the church. He couldn't just have people standing outside waiting to get in like some club on Friday night. He had to get Sunday School started. He tidied up the church, dusting a little here and there, changing last-minute light bulbs that would suddenly go out, polishing furniture, and before he started anything, he always began with a prayer. He took his pastoral duties seriously. He left nothing untouched or unsaved.

But I'm jumping ahead. Let me give you a little background information about us.

Do you want to hear a story about how a Baptist girl fell in love with a promising Pentecostal preacher from 4th Ward, Texas (a neighborhood in Houston, TX)? My parents were kind of like your typical love story. They were high school sweethearts, but we really should call them 4th Ward sweethearts. She and my dad's family knew of each other before they even started dating. They knew some of the same people. How my dad got my mom may seem stalkerish or, for some, a story out of a fairytale book, a very rare fairytale book. My dad used to follow my mom's school bus to my grandmother's house to see if she made it home safely. He even called random numbers from the phonebook to find my grandmother's number but eventually got the number from one of my mom's friends. Yes, a phonebook. Kids today probably think, what is a phonebook when I can just google? Back then, if you wanted a phone number, a phonebook was your Google. I call that hard work and dedication. He was determined and willing to jump hurdles for her. The funny thing is she didn't like my dad at first. She thought he was this weird man who wore cowboy boots in summertime. One night, while lying in bed, my mom prayed for the man she wanted, and the man she wanted was the man in her face already. They eventually got engaged, married, and had the four of us. Growing up in a household and having a healthy relationship to watch was beautiful. Having both parents together and married was a little uncommon where I lived. I always got asked if my dad was my stepdad or if my siblings and I were really siblings.

Before becoming pastor of our home church, my dad was a protégé, working under the founder and former head pastor, our great Uncle B. William, before he unfortunately passed away due to prostate cancer. He left the church behind to my dad. He was training him on what a pastor should be and what he stands for outside and inside the church. Just giving him the proper guidance to being a true man of God and learning more about the church business. Like I said before, my mama did not go to church with us. Being a little girl in church, of course, I should have been paying attention to the word of God. Instead, my mind was off, wondering. I would see the looks women would give my daddy, knowing this man was married with four kids. See me, Narah, I'm way more observant than my brothers. I'm a female. We females pay attention to every detail, big and small, and on top of that, I'm my mother's daughter. Nothing was getting by me.

Growing up, I would always feel weird that there would be women who weren't my mama being underneath my daddy. Every Sunday, asking him if he wanted this or that, giving him glasses full of his favorite Gatorade to drink. It would be nice and slushy; that is how he preferred it. One woman would always put a paper towel underneath his glass and fold it twice. She did the same thing every Sunday, like clockwork, but I had to quickly understand certain church members had specific roles, and nobody would steal my daddy. In the church, we called that ushering or a pastor's aid. That was important. If the pastor or another minister needed something on the pulpit, it was their duty to provide it. I didn't get it until I was older, though, because eventually, I would be in training to do the same thing. When you're a preacher's kid, understand that you will be very involved even when you don't want to. You are bound to get a church duty no matter how many times you ask why.

Luckily, some things were easily passed down to us. Emmanuel played the organ and keyboard like my daddy, aunt, and great-aunt. They all played by ear, simply catching the beat by a sound. Emmanuel even sang a little. I used to say I was forced to sing. I felt embarrassed and didn't like the fact the whole church was looking at me. I just closed my eyes and did my thing, but I secretly liked it. My daddy loved it, so I tried to do it with a smile. I would always chew gum to help with my nerves. Okay, chewing gum during service is like against the law in church. The second I began chewing, here came my daddy tip-toeing out the pulpit with a paper towel in hand, slowly making his way up to me. He stood right there and made me spit it out. Yeah, I laughed it off, but it was highly embarrassing. But I knew good and well I should not have been smacking on the mic like that.

Ezekiel was learning to play the drums while learning to play bass guitar, too, and Elijah was like a deacon and usher in training. When my brothers and I were off duty, we would also get caught sleeping. I would always peek over at the pulpit to see if my daddy was watching. I would look up, and he would be laughing. Although he meant business, he was just as silly as us.

As if napping while my daddy was preaching was not enough (you would think I got enough right). No, those after-church naps are just as serious as an after-school nap. As a child, you think there is nothing better than going home and going to sleep. It is not like we were the ones standing up preaching for hours and laying hands on people, but we were tired, too. Look, Sunday

School started at 9:00. Morning worship service, which was merged into the actual church service, started at 11:00. You had an altar call, or some people call it prayer time, and when that happens, you never know what the Holy Spirit will do. He can really take over the whole service at that point. Then you had giving time. "God loves what?" "A cheerful giver." Then, the church announcements and the benediction (benediction: an expression of good wishes; short blessings at the end of a religious service). And if we were lucky, church was out by 2:00. Don't get me wrong, we loved church. We love it even more now that we are older. But if your daddy was a pastor, preacher, or any type of minister of a church, it was never really over. Just because he was done and down from that pulpit meant nothing.

You have those who would wait around to hug the pastor just to say a simple "thank you" for the word he just preached, an extra private prayer request, or those who just wanted to talk. Do not get me wrong, my brothers and I knew this was our daddy's lifestyle. We did not mind sharing him. This was a job that God called him to do. Being a pastor did not end on Sundays, and we respected that. I mean, we were kids, so did we really have a choice? This was his first job, away from his second job. Luckily, we had our pickles and peppermint candy to keep us company, thanks to our Aunt Mildred, Uncle Benjamin's wife. She would bring hot dogs and cookies to have every Sunday. I mean, she never missed a beat. Our Aunt Mildred was a true pillar, I tell you. She was this tall, bright, red-haired, curly-wearing afro woman who was on fire for God. You knew it, too, whenever the beat was slow at church, or she needed you to keep up with her because she was getting happy (feeling the Holy Spirit or an uncontrollable feeling of the Holy Ghost). (Holy Spirit: third person in the holy trinity, comforter.) She would get up from her seat standing next to the organ and beat it like a drum, and she was not afraid to correct you about us four. She was quick with it, too.

But back to trying to leave church on time. We would be in the car buckled up, ready to go, radio on, air on. So you think you're in the clear? Nope. Next thing you know, you hear, "Pastor, let me ....." or "Pastor, can I ....." Then, before you know it, another conversation picks up. It's a deep one. Thirty minutes later, the convo is going strong. Then you hear the famous line, "Okay. Alright, Pastor. Let me let you go so you can get these kids home because I know the first lady got a nice meal waiting for ya'll at the house." But then the convo picks back up because they start talking about my mother's dishes and what she was making for dessert. My mama had a book of all different types of recipes, so we were for sure eating good every day. My friends would always pick on me about "living at church" because it always took us a while to get home. They would always say things like, "Man, does church last that long for real? If so, we are never trying to go." Funny enough, eventually, I ended up bringing most of them to church, or some of them would even bring their Bible to my door and ask for my dad because they had a question.

Once we got home, all we wanted to do was play outside or take another nap until dinner was ready. My daddy insisted that Sundays were just for family time. On a typical Sunday, we would drop someone off at home, then pick up a little snack from Burger King and go to the store for last-minute dinner things or something extra needed for the week. He would come home, change into his white beater, and turn on The Word Network (more preaching for the preacher). He would watch his favorite Bishop G.E Patterson. Then came this huge meal of meatloaf with gravy, a pot of spiced ranch-style pinto beans, cabbage with rice, and cornbread. The dessert was a peach cobbler with vanilla ice cream. So, when I tell you we were eating, honey, I mean we were eating.

Chapter 2

WE THE FAMILY

I know everyone has their little jokes and sayings about preachers' kids. The world loves to give preachers' kids a bad reputation. Even the media does it sometimes. The world often has this narrative of how a preacher's life should be, from his wife and kids down to house, car, and clothes. Not every pastor is out here in a private plane, jet, or house with ten bedrooms, twelve golden toilets, iced jewelry from head to toe, and thousand-dollar suits. Now, look, if you are a man or woman of God and you're reading this, I'm not saying there is something wrong if you have these things. If God blessed you well enough to have that lifestyle, live on. Don't be ashamed because there is nothing wrong with enjoying what God blessed you with. God wants his children to live well. I'm just saying that's not every pastor's reality. But that is the only perception the world has. When they see or hear the word preacher, they think of shiny suits and yelling in a mic for dollars. God is not about a paycheck. He is about your soul and your love for Him and others. It is our duty as children of God to give to the house of God. Why? Well, because if your home (the place you eat and sleep) needed work done, wouldn't you fix it? The money we give to God's house is for God's house. Taking care of your place of fellowship and worship, where you get fed and giving to the poor, is also caring for God's house. So, to the world, not every pastor is physically rich. There are plenty who go to work Monday through Friday. And a fun fact: some pastors put most of their own money into the church.

We lived a pretty middle-class life. My dad had a nine-to-five outside of church that he went to every day. We went to a public school. My mama didn't spend her days going on shopping sprees or taking expensive trips. We fought like normal siblings and got whippings like normal kids or like most kids. From elementary school up to middle school, I remember being called a preacher's kid and getting made fun of because of it. I was the kid who blasted gospel music in her handphones and got picked on for it. I was a person who was bullied, and eventually, I became the bully. I always felt like I had to prove myself by fighting.

Being told that I could not or would not fight because of who my daddy was kind of left me thinking, *show them*. My brothers and I knew how to lay hands, and I'm not talking about just praying. I did not want to be that way, but sometimes, things happen. We can get angry. Look, even Jesus flipped the table. At times, it could feel like we were being watched under a microscope, and we could not do anything out of order. When certain church members found out we did or were doing something we had no business doing, baby, that's it. Your name is now quickly added to the prayer request box and will be mentioned on the prayer request line. That meant the old church mothers who carried candy, tissue, and an extra prayer cloth in their purse were about to pray the house down and scream your name to the heavens.

I always hear people say, "Oh, church folks are some of the messiest and rudest people," which turns them off to church. Well, although this may be true, that's not the case in every church. But you also got messy people on your job. So, are you still going? You do have some people waiting for the preacher's kid to act a fool or get caught in foolery just so they can say, "I told you so." They could run and tell the organ player and deacon down to the missionary, and then you will begin hearing whispers. You have some people that think preachers' kids cannot do anything. They used to think our parents locked us up in a closet, reading the Bible nonstop. Or they use the Bible as punishment like they do in the movies. Of course, we had at-home Bible Study and prayer time, but our parents gave us freedom. We could go to the mall and movies. We could spend time together with friends. Church kids aren't just caged in; we were taught to always carry ourselves a certain way because of who we are in God. Having fun doesn't equal hell-bound. It's just the type of fun you have. We laugh. We joke. I mean, we are very much human. Just because we choose not to do certain things doesn't mean we are better than or perfect or bougie, but we are God's people, so we are called to be different.

Now, you don't have to walk around screaming it to the rooftops or put an "I love Jesus" bumper sticker on your car. It's just a light you carry. People should see you and see God. The joy and light you carry should rub off on someone who may not know God, and because of you, they want to know Him. I think almost every household could agree with this when it came to sleeping over at a friend's. That was an absolute, flat-out no. I mean, don't even fix your mouth to ask. We didn't participate in Halloween either. One year, I called myself trying to go trick or treating with my friends. Yes, it was behind my parents' back. We went to a neighborhood nearby. There were these guys dressed in all black chasing us throughout the neighborhood, and as soon as I took off running, I fell hard on the ground right on my side. I wondered if God was looking at me, saying, "See, you shouldn't have been disobedient. Now get home." We also didn't watch the movies where people were possessed by evil spirits and cast spells and talked to dead people because that stuff was real, and my mama and daddy did not play those games with us. They would say, "Be careful with what you watch and listen to. Your eyes are the windows to your soul. And watch the people you hang around; everybody isn't your friend." One of the reasons she did not let us go to everybody's house is because you just do not know what everybody is into. You never really know what somebody is doing behind closed doors. Spirits are real, and they move from person to person. She also did not let us eat everybody's cooking, especially if we knew they did not like us.

Growing up, of course, I was upset and didn't understand why we could not do certain things. But as I got older, especially the age I am now with a child of my own, I get it. This world is changing every day and getting more evil. My parents grew up in a time when you could leave your front door open and not worry about somebody running up in your place. If they knew whose kid you were and if you were out acting a fool, they were running to tell your mama and daddy.

Unfortunately, that world does not exist anymore sadly. You got parents fighting. Kids fighting parents. The stuff that most of these young kids are doing today, my generation did not dare do. Honestly, we were just too scared to try it anyway.

My brothers and I were starting to grow up. I mean, we could not stay kids forever, right? We were not those little quiet church kids anymore. At times, people were shocked at the things that came out of our mouths. Not because it was disrespectful. It was more like, *wow, those kids are really growing up.* I mean, they have known us since we were babies. They would always compliment us on how sweet and well-dressed we were. We were a reflection of both parents, and it seemed like we each got a fair equal part of our parents' personality in us. Emmanuel was a little bit of the more peaceful, non-confrontational type. Now, he was cool until you pissed him off, then he had a temper like my PawPaw. I was the shy one and noticeably quiet. I did not really like being around people, and please don't make me angry because my mama's not-so-good side will come out of me. Look, I'm very short. So you know I have a short fuse already. My mouth was very much ready to cut you. When it came to the twins, they were very mellow, cool dudes. They were the type to get disappointed and just simply not want to deal with you. We were all chill kids until you made us upset. I guess we got our temper and sense of protection for one another from our parents. Honestly, I never really saw our dad lose his cool. Until one day, I had to tell my parents that I was sexually violated by a classmate while coming home from school. That was one of the hardest things I had to do - tell my dad his only daughter had forcefully been touched. I saw his eyes filled with rage. The next day, he came up to my school, and it was like the Hulk unleashed himself. Jesus had to be sitting in the principal's office that day because that was the only thing that kept my daddy from placing his hands around the boy's neck.

When it came to our parents protecting us, you would start to see the other side of them. We were not going to allow anyone to pick on one of us, especially when it came to Elijah, who is number three out of the four of us who also has autism. How is living with someone with autism? Well, I'll say this: everybody is not the same when it comes to autism. You had some that were verbal and some non-verbal. Elijah was just like any other regular person, and we tried not to treat him any differently. He knew how to cook, use the microwave, wash dishes, and use basic cleaning tools. He knew how to google almost everything. His memory was better than any of ours. If you told him you were going to do something, make sure you kept your word because he would remind you. His organizational skills were top-tier, especially if it had anything to do with his many collections of different color Sharpie pens. People often assume if someone has autism, they cannot do any daily tasks. Although there are various levels of autism, that does not mean they are not competent or can not beat life's challenges. They are smart in other ways you would not even think of. They are great listeners and a little bit nosey, too. It is like God gave them a different type of intelligence. Now, do not think we were around here being some gang or something, but we just wanted to protect each other.

Monday through Friday, my dad went to work. On Tuesdays, he would be at church for Bible Study and prayer. He would even go to people's homes or the hospital to pray for them. He would also take people to the grocery store throughout the week after work.

Sometimes, we went to extra services where he had to preach, and of course, we had to be there. But that is why we called him our Superman. He had a thousand jobs but was still strong and able enough to do all of them; even on his off days, he still was a busy man. He was a marriage counselor, a pastor, a preacher, and most of all, a husband and father, all while having one child with autism and two with diabetes who needed daily medication to move throughout the day. I watched my daddy pray for my grandmother, who had a condition called MS (Multiple Sclerosis: nerve damage that disrupts communication between the brain and body). Every time we went over to my grandmother's, he would lay hands over her legs with holy oil, and she would be able to walk down her hallway to her den without the need for a walker. That was the gift that God blessed him with. He would always say he was in the business of saving souls, and we have seen it firsthand.

We were not rich, but we had everything we needed. We were a middle-class family, but our parents made sure we never ever went without. Every year, when Christmas time came, we had to write four things we wanted. We always got a little something on Christmas day, but the real gifts came in February. We could get a little now and more later. Yes, I'm talking about tax time. If you know, you know. He also most certainly made sure that we knew Christmas was about Jesus. He made sure that we knew holidays like Easter, as well, were all about Jesus. As a matter of fact, we now say Resurrection Sunday. He told us that there was no such thing as a bunny hopping around laying different colored eggs, and there was no fat, jolly man in a red suit with reindeer coming down a chimney with a bag of gifts in his hands. Plus, we did not even have a chimney. I mean, of course, we were children, but our parents kept it very real with us.

I can't recall a time one of us cried because we found out the tooth fairy or Santa Claus or the easter bunny was not real. But that is because of the foundation our parents built for us. They were not going to feed us a lie or fairytale. We knew our daddy worked hard, made the money, and brought those gifts. Our parents' goal was not to mislead us. This may sound harsh and boring to some, but not to us. We had our family traditions. We would listen to our local radio station's Christmas music around the clock, starting from Thanksgiving all the way to Christmas Eve. We jammed the radio all the way through the house. We watched classic Christmas movies with our daddy. We decorated our home. We had a Christmas tree and hung lights. My mama even stayed up all Christmas Eve baking cakes and cookies. Yes, we did it up. It might seem corny to some, but we genuinely looked forward to it every year.

A dresser. My daddy was a dresser. He had the suits and the shoes to match. He loved a nice pair of Stacey Adams shoes and a nice shiny watch on his wrist. Sometimes, on Saturdays after the Sabbath service was over (yes, we went to church Saturday to Sabbath service, which was basically, in my opinion, a small conversation about the Bible. So, like a Bible Study, I guess there wasn't any music or anything, just talking.) we would head over to one of his favorite stores, The Suit Mart. They had everything down to shirts, hats, belts, shoes, wallets, and jewelry. That was his spot It was like a mega-suit mall. He made sure the robes that he wore on particular Sundays were nice and fresh. He had a purple and black one that was always crisp. That one was my favorite. He had an all-white robe for communion. He would wear a black button-down shirt with a white collar. He had this big silver cross that he tucked into the pocket of his shirt. (Communion: an act done every first Sunday in remembrance of Christ's death until the day He comes back, which consists of a small cracker and grape juice or wine. The wine or grape juice represents the blood that Jesus shed, and the cracker or communion bread represents the body.)

If I could describe his preaching style, it was as hard as a punch with a little funny sense of humor to it in a way. He kind of reminded us of one of his favorites, Bishop G.E Patterson. Our daddy was an old-school Pentecostal preacher. I liked the fact that he would put jokes into sermons. Honestly, as a small child sitting in church all those hours, it kept me awake. He would often add us and my mama into his sermons as well. He was putting some flavor into it. He was long-winded, but once again, I was a small child, so of course, they seemed long. Still, now that I am older, I can say I appreciate a long sermon, but nothing too lengthy. Still, hey, you can never have enough of Jesus. We have grown to long for those long sermons, altar calls, and foot-stomping types of church. When you're a kid, and you know Jesus, you are told of His works and His forgiveness, but when you're grown and going through this thing called life, you begin to understand Jesus and grow a love for God and have your own personal relationship with Him. The prayers were long and strong, and we felt it. Once the holy oil was placed on your forehead and the Holy Spirit hit you, it was something you wanted to hold on to forever. The things we witnessed in that church groomed us for life. We know the Holy Spirit is real, and once He came in, He stayed in until somebody got just what they wanted from the Lord: to be set free, to be made over and restored. The casting out of ungodly spirits and getting purged was real. Especially if someone was running from God when the Spirit came in, it was like that game of tag you'd been playing with God was over because He finally got a hold of you. Let me tell you how serious it was. Our Aunt Mildred would tell us to close our eyes and pray in the name of Jesus and keep our minds on Him. She put Bibles on our stomachs to cover us while this was going on. People love to think church is just a game or a get-rich scheme. No, God is real. The enemy is real, and he uses people to try and get his agenda out. We belonged to a church where if your skirts were short, those mothers would come by you and shamelessly place a prayer cloth over your legs. It's just rare to find a church like that now. It's nothing like an old-school church with a good praise break.

We knew there was a difference between the pastor and dad. The approach was only slightly different. My older brother and his long-term girlfriend turned fiancé were expecting a baby. You know how in those movies where they show the parents disowning their children or kicking them out of the home because they had a baby out of wedlock and giving the "this is an abomination to God" speech? Nope, that was not happening. He was not about to use that pulpit to turn his back on his son. God has His way. We want to do things our way. One of God's reasons, for sure, is to protect us from any harm, danger or hurt that could come from us doing it our way. But sometimes, we often turn away from His will and follow our own.

But He knows His children. He even knows the number of hairs on your head. So, trust me, before you did it your way, He knew you would. That is why He offers us the gift of forgiveness, and our lives are not over. There is always a blessing in every lesson, and He still loves us. God's will is perfect for you. Some church folks can be rude or chatty in these types of situations. Some could genuinely mean well, but the delivery is off, maybe just simply wanting better for you but not knowing how to say it. My mama had this saying, "You could quote bible verses all day, but is your house clean?" The difference between people and God is that when you fall, people laugh. But with God, He picks you up and dusts you off, and guess what? Not just once, He will dust you off each time you fall.

Think of it this way. Jesus is your teammate. You are in a basketball game. God is the coach, Jesus is your point guard, and the Holy Spirit is the ref. There are ten seconds left in the fourth quarter. What are you going to do? Let the enemy score or consult your teammate and win the victory because, at the end of the day, God's got your back.

Emmanuel and his longtime girlfriend were expecting their first child together. So, the whole church knew he was about to be a father. One Sunday morning, my daddy politely addressed what was already obvious. He let the people know what was and what was not. After he was done with his sermon before the benediction, he stood up in the pulpit. He made it clear that Emmanuel was his son, and whatever they spoke about concerning the situation was dealt with in private between him, my mama, and God. He did not want anyone to judge them or beat them down. He spoke about how everybody has a past and how everybody in the building was not saved all their life. Everybody had a different life before finding Jesus, so I think, in a way, he was trying to protect them. I am pretty sure there were whispers and talks at people's dinner tables about what was going on, but I am glad my dad set it in stone that nobody was going to beat his children down. Just because he did that, it did not mean he stood for what they did, but there is a thing that God gives us called grace, mercy, and forgiveness. And honestly, we must give the same to others. Sometimes, we can be our hardest critics.

We are not here on earth to live for the glory of people but for the glory of God. You can't please everyone, and if you try, you will never be happy. God has a purpose for every one of us. We should not beat each other up, especially as followers of Christ. We should all strive to be Christ-like. We are representations of God for other people to see His light shine through us so we can help bring somebody to Christ. If God gave up on us every time we stepped out of His will, we would be in trouble. Babies are gifts from God and a blessing. This does not make you any less than in God's sight. He loves us. God forgives and does not remember. People forgive and will bring it up any chance they get.

Chapter 3

THE NEW NORMAL IS HERE

*W*e should all know life is precious. It is something that should not be taken lightly. But sadly, we do. We sometimes take even the smallest things for granted, like making it home from the store or making it back home safe from a nice walk around the park. We should never forget to thank God. To wake up every day is a blessing. Everything in this life should be celebrated as a blessing, like a woman carrying a baby. That new life forming inside her is a blessing. Every birthday we have is a blessing because someone didn't make it home or did not make it to their next birthday.

I could keep going, but you get the point. Of course, God wants us to enjoy life, but we should remember we do not know which day is our last. Love while you can, and appreciate life while you can. Never walk around ungrateful or holding a grudge. Life is just too short. We have presidents, mayors, and governors, but Jesus is in control of all things. He gives us free will but still holds the original plans. He takes things meant for evil and uses them for good. Sometimes, life is hard and unfair, and it is very unpredictable. It could bring you down when you least expect it sometimes. We do not understand why God allows certain things to happen to us. And sometimes it hurts, and it sucks, and it feels like God has left you, or He just doesn't hear your prayers any more, but that isn' true. He will not leave you nor abandon you. God is a God that cannot and will not lie. No matter how alone you feel and no matter who will or will not pick up the phone for you. God will not leave you. God will always answer your call.

Now, it was my last year of high school, and Elijah and Ezekiel were getting ready to enter their third. It was time for things like prom, graduation, learning how to drive, and filling out college applications for some. My older brother now had three little ones and a place of his own with his fiancé. The next step would be moving out of our three-bedroom apartment into a home. Things were starting to move forward, but then suddenly, it seemed as if this thing called life took a pause, I mean a long pause.

It was Saturday afternoon; there was no Sabbath service this weekend and no errands to run. Everyone was just sitting around enjoying the weekend, lounging around the house. My mom and dad called us into their bedroom. I was thinking, *man, someone did something, and now we are all in trouble*. I remember my dad turning his head as if he had a painful crook in his neck. I mean, he could barely move it. He had to turn his whole body just to look at us. He looked at us with a smile on his face; now, my dad was a huge joker. The size of his laugh said it all, but you could see by the look on my mother's face this was not a joke.

Before the conversation started, I ran to my room, remembering I had my senior pictures taken a few days before. Walking back into my parent's room, I hurried and showed them. He began to cry while looking at my picture, but I was not sure if he was joking or not. The first thing he told us was not to worry. Isn't it weird the moment someone tells us not to worry, that's when the worrying starts? And with no sadness, no tears, no anger, and no fear in his eyes, he told us he was sick. We knew our dad had been battling with things like high blood pressure since he was in high school, but he took meds for that, so what could he mean? My mind raced quietly. This did not seem like it was about something simple like a cold or even the flu. He would not tell us anything common like that. He went on to say, "First, I do not have cancer. The tumor has cancer." *TUMOR?!? CANCER?!? WAIT!!* My siblings and I were in shock. I mean, time froze. The only thing I ever heard about cancer is that it makes you small and you lose a lot of weight and your hair. Some say it is a battle for your life. We knew our Aunt Phillis, my mother's sister, was a breast cancer survivor. I do not think at the time we had that much to say. I mean, what exactly do you say to that? It is a scary feeling. Honestly, never in my life did I ever think something like this would happen to our dad. I am not sure if we knew how to process the information yet. As I mentioned before, we did not have too much knowledge about this thing called cancer. We also knew there was a chance of survival. You could beat this and live a long life. It takes people through different stages, and each stage takes you through something different. We hoped that maybe it was caught early, and once they removed his tumor, he would be back to normal. I couldn't see anything like this getting him down. I remember one Sunday in church; our daddy mentioned that at an early age, he was told he wasn't supposed to live that long due to a condition he had as a child, so if he could beat that, he for sure could beat this thing called cancer.

Stage four! Stage four! How could it already be at stage four? It was stage four thyroid cancer. It was one of the most aggressive types of thyroid cancer, but how? Why was it at the last stage already? Like, is there a last stage I forgot to google about? It did not make any sense. He was young, healthy, loving, and caring. He was always willing to go out of his way to help someone else. People like him do not just get sick. They pray the sickness away. We did not understand. He was a pastor, a God-fearing man who took care of his family and church, and a true provider. I wondered why it had to be him. He was a true example of a man. He took care of his family; he provided us with everything we needed. Even though I never asked her, I knew my mama had to be sacred and worried. I often wondered who she cried to and how she remained strong.

Things seemed to change overnight. His voice went from strong and mighty like a lion to faint, hoarse, and raspy. It sounded like he had been screaming for days and finally lost his voice. It was more like a whisper when he spoke. Then his weight was leaving him, and we could tell. Our dad was a pretty big guy. He wore a baseball cap because his hair started slowly falling out, and his appearance was completely different. He went from big and strong to fragile; it was heartbreaking. I didn't like how he was preparing us for his absence. Then again, I thought maybe the things he was teaching were only normal things you learn as you get older. He could not drive anymore or hardly write because the chemotherapy was affecting his ability to do certain things. (Chemotherapy: a treatment that uses powerful chemicals to kill fast-growing cells in the body.) This was designed to help fight off cancer, but it seemed like it made him sicker and look sicker. He would stay in treatment for a certain amount of hours. Sometimes, Emmanuel and I would go with him. He would sit there most of the day watching "In the Heat of the Night" reruns. Even in his pain, going through his battle, he didn't forget his calling.

He never went around shouting from the rooftop that he was a pastor. He was there getting chemo like everybody else. People just knew they saw God's light shining on him. Look, I said before, you don't have to wear a t-shirt saying I'm a follower of Christ. It is about the light you have. He saw fit to forget about himself for a moment and pray for those who were also in chemo. The day he rang that bell meant chemo was complete. My brothers and I would take turns walking to the store for my dad. That was our way of helping out, and honestly, it felt good to know our parents could depend on us.

He did not want anyone to know how sick he was. He did not even want us to know; he kept a lot of things from us during his time of sickness. I can recall one night, my mother called me into their bedroom. I saw him lying there on the floor on the side of their bed, weak. He couldn't move. I wasn't sure if he accidentally rolled out of bed or stood up and fell while getting up out of bed. I just slowly helped him get back in bed. It was terrifying; we didn't want to see him this way. You could tell at times his strength was leaving him. Of course, he could still talk and laugh.

It was good to know he still found a moment where he could laugh.

When out in public, he had to carry a white Styrofoam cup with him. He had this dry cough, which made him often cough up blood and other fluids. I hated how much people would stare at him when he had to use it. Sometimes, he laughed too hard. He would have to clutch his throat tight because it was painful. One day, while in the grocery store picking up his meds, this guy insisted on keeping his eyes on my daddy because he had to use his cup. Now, when he used it, he never did those big, nasty clearing of the throat sounds like someone with bad sinuses. You really would not know what he was doing with that cup unless you were staring at him a little too hard.

I am glad my dad's sense of humor was still with him. He tapped me on my shoulder and pointed at the man looking at him, and I turned with the meanest look on my face and shouted, "Boo," in a funny way. Of course, my daddy (he never sits back and allows me to bully someone) laughed and looked at me and said, "You so stupid." If you made him laugh and he called you that, it was a good thing, more of a term of endearment.

Church went from every Sunday to every other Sunday to sometimes staying at home to not coming any longer. But whenever he did go to church, he did not sit on the pulpit. Things like using his voice were wearing him down. He could not preach anymore. His suits and robes became too big for him. Watching him have to sit out was weird. Not weird, but it was not normal. Although he could no longer make it to church, he made sure we went so we would catch the bus to and from church. We would get rides to the bus stop after church or sometimes just have a ride all the way home. Now you are wondering why we did not have a ride there. We were the pastor's kids. Look, honestly, I could not tell you I am not sure. Even to this day, I'm not sure why nobody was obligated to give us rides, and most of the members were on the bus line themselves. We knew preaching was something that he loved to do, and watching him take a step back from everything hurt.

One day in late December, he was in severe pain and refused to go to the hospital. We had to call some reinforcement, our Uncle Luke, our dad's older brother, who unfortunately is no longer with us. He stood a little bit over six feet tall. I mean, he had to bend down a little so he could get into our apartment. Eventually, he finally gave in, and we all helped him put shoes and socks on. Emmanuel and his fiancé, Mia, took him. He stayed in the hospital for a while. My mom looked so sad. She did not have to say anything to us about her feelings. Sometimes, a person can tell you how they feel without saying anything. You could feel that she was hurting and fighting back her fear and tears.

A few days became a few weeks. It was always a house full of six, never a dull moment, but suddenly it seemed empty, not really any laughter, just TVs playing and the house phone ringing off the hook constantly. We went to visit him, but knowing that this person was not coming home with you sucked. It did not feel right leaving him there. I wondered how alone he felt. Were the doctors and nurses letting him rest? Were they poking him too much with things? He called the house when he could, which was often; we were hoping and praying he would come home soon. My mother was asked if she wanted to put our dad on a morphine drip. NO!

She said no, but of course, in hospital fashion, they did it anyway without her consent. Why did a morphine drip seem like such a terrible idea? Well, it was an extremely strong pain medication. Some say morphine is the last-call drug. He had this huge mask on his face hooked up to this machine. It seemed so heavy on him. Sitting there watching him look so little was the worst; it looked like his body was sinking into the bed. It was not fair. We needed him home again. This was our Superman. I felt an unexpected tear roll down my cheek. My older brother was so hurt that he couldn't stand being in the room any longer. No one wants to see the person they love, especially a parent, in a state like that. Your emotions are everywhere. You don't know what to think. His nurse came into his hospital room and let us know he was sedated so he could hear us talking to him, but he couldn't respond. I just sat there quietly. I did not want to speak. Really, I just did not know what to say. What do you say in that situation? I just looked at him, but we just knew after all this that God was going to heal him. He was not going to die. There was just no way. It was not possible.

January 6th, the phone kept ringing and ringing. From the sounds of my eavesdropping, it sounded like it could be one of the nurses from the hospital. They were asking my mama to gather the family; nobody was accepting that at all. My dad always had a fighting spirit in him. I mean, he beat this condition that he had when he was a child. And he wasn't expected to live long. He made it all the way to the age of forty-three with a wife, kids, and grandchildren. I mean, he made it, so he was going to beat this surely. It was in his blood already to fight. He was not about to give up. He was not leaving us. My aunt called him a modern-day

Job because no matter how much of his strength was leaving him, no matter how much the cancer was spreading throughout his body, Dad always gave God the glory. He stayed faithful to God's word and never let go of His hand. We were not about to give up. We kept praying and believing in God. The circumstances looked bad, but we knew the type of God we served.

Knowing I should not be trying to sneak and listen in on conversations, I honestly did not hear that much but heard enough. I ran to the room and thought as positively as I could, saying my best prayer, begging God to save his life and begging God for a miracle. I knew the power of prayer could change things, but I wish I could have prayed longer and had more faith in God. My mama and Aunt Bethany got together and went to work and called a congregation of preachers, pastors, bishops, all men of faith, and men that could pray heaven down and believe in what they were praying about, asking God to move this mountain and heal our daddy. My mind started going all over the place, wondering if it was a terrible thing that they were coming together at this moment or if something bad was happening.

Everyone was shocked. No one knew how sick he was. No one knew things had gotten bad like this. Most of them did not even know he had cancer. Even though it was apparent he was sick, some people did not know, but that is how my dad wanted it. He did not want everyone to know how sick he was; even to this day, I still do not know why. I honestly think if it were up to him, we still would not know. He would have suffered in silence. His oxygen levels were getting low. He was put on a breathing machine, and doctors wanted to test and see if he could breathe on his own. At some point, they would be removing him from the machine. My thing is, as a doctor, why would you make plans to remove someone from a machine that's giving him oxygen if you know the outcome couldn't be better? My mother asked them not to remove him, just give him more time, but that is the health care system for you.

The cancer started to spread to his brain. My father was no longer working and was forced into early retirement due to his sickness, which meant no insurance. There were plans to remove the tumor from his brain, but that's the way of the world. You can work in this world all your life, and the minute you can't, they just toss you aside. And the moment you don't have the proper funds, no matter if you're on your deathbed or not, they can't do anything for you. Hospitals are supposed to help the sick. Still, we must remember it's also a business. Hospitals make a lot of money. Unfortunately, my daddy was misdiagnosed a few times. They could've caught this early; more could've been done. With these men and women of God praying and our faith (I mean, the Bible says you need the faith of a mustard seed), we knew in our hearts God was going to heal him.

Chapter 4

JANUARY CAME

*J*anuary 7th .... My brothers and I were getting dressed to go to see my dad at the hospital. This was the second day the phone would ring off the hook. Now, I had no choice but to be nosey, thinking, *who could be calling like this*? Back-to-back. I decided to walk into my parents' bathroom, pretending to get something I needed. On the way out, I stopped at the door frame to listen. I got the feeling she was on the phone with the hospital again. And honestly, this is something I really did not need to hear. I went back to my room, but this time, I panicked without really knowing any information, but I could hear it in my mom's small response. I tried so hard to shake off any doubt and worry that I had in my head. I just repeated over and over, "He's going to be okay, he's going to be okay," because I thought if you think negative thoughts and plant that seed, it would grow. So, I needed to think happy, positive thoughts. Because honestly, I did not know if it was good or bad news. Putting the fear of the unknown behind me, I continued getting dressed.

I walked back into my mother's room, this time needing something. She was back on the phone again. All I could remember hearing was, "Okay, uh huh." She ended the conversation with, "Okay, we are on the way, Thank you." On the ride to the hospital, my mind kept running everywhere, thinking about what could have happened. My mama did not say much on the ride there. So, I just assumed everything was good. We finally made it, but as soon as we got out of the parking garage, we saw some of our dad's preacher friends. It triggered me because nobody ever really came up to visit on the same day as us. Even before reaching the room, fear hit me again, and it was the simplest thing. It was the way they hugged and comforted my mama. They looked like something was wrong. They hugged her for too long. It looked like they were consoling her. I'm pretty sure it worried my brothers, too. There was a hallway that led to the waiting room. I noticed family members, friends, and ex-church members standing there. They were all crying with their heads down, and all looked like they wanted to run up and hug us.

My mama had not said anything just yet. I was thinking it had to be extremely serious if everyone was up here. Or maybe they just found out how sick he was, and they all would come together and pray. My mama stopped us before we got too deep into the waiting room. She looked at us as she burst into tears. In a high-pitched voice, the first words she said were, "I'm sorry ya'll. He's gone. He didn't make it. We stopped immediately and started to cry. Elijah fell straight to his knees in disbelief. Emmanuel was shocked, confused, and left to gather himself and process what he had just heard. I just don't think he was able to handle it. We all had a tight connection with our dad, but Emmanuel was his firstborn. I remember hearing stories from our family members that he and Dad went everywhere together. They had a connection with playing the organ. All I could do was run to the nearest bathroom and cry. I didn't get it. Our Uncle Luke actually ran into the women's restroom, trying to console us. Pulling myself together, I walked arm in arm with my mother down the long lobby, going into his room. I did not know what to do. I would not be angry because certain people were not family and should not have been allowed in that room. I needed to focus on the fact that we just lost our daddy. My siblings and I had to be strong for our mama. There he was, right there, my eyes connected to him, looking at Ezekiel standing there over our daddy's body, crying. We were all so emotional. My mama could not even explain to him what happened. I do not think, at that moment, any of us wanted to process anything yet.

At first, I didn't want to look at him; I just wanted to put my head down, but there he was right in front of me. I was hoping and pleading in my head that he would suddenly gasp for air, and the machine would start making sounds, and lights would start flashing, showing signs of life. *He will wake up. The doctors are wrong. The Lord will show us a miracle.* I looked extra hard at his stomach, trying to see if he would start breathing again. In my mind, I thought I saw his stomach move. I did not want to believe I was standing there. Like, *God, please show us a miracle.* Sadly, we as humans will never fully understand why certain things happen to certain people, good people. I must be honest. I never once thought about a day without my parents being here. Hearing my mama cry and blame herself for something she had no say in was heartbreaking. She was saying how she should have done more.

Our mother was broken, and broken may not even be the word. But if I could put a word to it, it would be broken. Seeing my dad's older cousins, who are all men of God, down to pastor, preacher, minister, and evangelist. I watched them fall into the bed with my dad with a face full of tears in disbelief.

You know, some people believe their loved ones pass away because God is punishing them or something like that. It's not true. Yes, it feels terrible. The feeling of losing a loved one is unmatched, a never-ending pain. God was not punishing us. He wasn't mad because we did not do enough. He saw his child in pain. He saw him suffering, so he chose to take him home. He was living the last few months of his life in pain. We asked for healing, and I believe wholeheartedly that he got it. It just wasn't meant for this earth. I wish I would've spoken and stood up and walked over to my mama instead of looking at her across the room. I was standing next to someone who, in my mind, didn't need to be there. After most of the room cleared, we were pulled into a prayer. A prayer that honestly no one in that room wanted to pray, and on top of that, I felt like you should've been praying. He's already gone, and I didn't feel like praying at that moment on that day. The prayer didn't move anything or anyone. I'm not sure why it was happening. I love to pray. It's the first thing I do in the morning and the last thing I do before bed. It could've just been the person that was saying the prayer. My sadness quickly turned into anger. Not only was it the setting, I thought about the unnecessary drama she brought to my dad right after he came out of open heart surgery. His stitches were still fresh. This is the same one that wanted to pray.

I thought, *how unbelievable is this?* I mean, he was fresh out of surgery, like in recovery. She was there to complain about church stuff. There was a service she attended at our church a few Sundays prior. I'm pretty sure that wasn't her intention, but why even bring it up? That could've been something talked about much later down the line. She brought up food. She talked about how the portion size was too small and the food was cold. Was that something really important after open heart surgery? My dad's tumor was big and went from his thyroid to his heart. So imagine yourself fresh out of surgery, and the first thing you hear about is some food someone didn't like. Honestly, I do not know why she did what she did. Maybe just don't eat the food or go home and heat it and keep that comment to yourself. If she only knew how much that hurt him, truly. And now you're grabbing me, wanting to pray. I didn't want to hear it. All I could think about was, *shut up, shut up, get your hands off me.*

After the family left, it should've just been us, his wife and kids. There were a few people in that lobby who weren't family and shouldn't have been allowed in his room at all until my mother made it there and allowed them in. I have done some growing. You know, I lived life and got a little wiser and have forgiven them. God nor my dad would want me holding on to that hurt because if he were still living, he would've forgiven them, too. We weren't ready to accept the fact he was gone. We stayed until they were ready to remove his body. Emmanuel stood over him, talking to him, shaking his shoulder, wanting him to open his eyes, repeatedly saying, "You said you would fight." We had to let his body go. It was hypoxemic oxygen respiratory failure, which meant there was not enough oxygen in his blood. It was secondary to metastatic thyroid cancer.

This is the thing: my daddy had received a threatening message one day from an ex-church member. They were already not a part of the church anymore. They wanted to cause physical harm to him and were disrespecting his wife and kids because of a big ego. They believed they deserved a certain title in the church. Some people in the church believe that a pastor is just supposed to hand it to them because they tell them to. They were even going to other churches extremely close to us, complaining because my dad didn't give them a title. See, my daddy wasn't going to put your business out there, but that didn't mean he wasn't going to sit you down if you were out in the club shaking like Shake and Bake. You want a title, but you were out living wild. Our daddy wasn't that type of pastor. He didn't just let anyone in his pulpit. He was just a no-nonsense preacher. So, I didn't get how these same people were crying over his lifeless body. It just seemed so fake to me. You should treat people right while they are living. I am sure they were sad and hurt that he passed away. I wondered if they ever apologized to him for the things they said and did. Were you crying and carrying on out of hurt, or was it guilt? Our dad gave his cancer battle a name - no weapon formed against me shall prosper (Isaiah 57:17).

I do not think things hit us right away. You are just there in the moment with everything. You are there in your head a lot. You are mad, you are sad, you are hurt, confused, frustrated. And the thing is, you cannot pick which emotion you want to feel. It just sneaks up on you. The old church saints say when another saint leaves, they're being called home, and their work on this earth was completed. They fulfilled their purpose here. Their mission is complete. The soul leaves, but the body stays here. To be absent from the body is to be present with the Lord (2 Corinthians 5:8). Everyone was put on this earth to do something, whether you believe that or not. Everyone has work to do. God didn't put us here for nothing.

You have to get used to not seeing the person you spent all your life with no longer being here. I thought of my mama more than I thought of myself. She spent every day since high school with him. Life was different. She couldn't call him, she couldn't see him, she couldn't randomly call him at work, and she couldn't smell his loud cologne throughout the apartment. We couldn't come home from school anymore and see him eating Pappa BBQ, or Denny's with my mama in the living room because he took off work early to enjoy the afternoon with his wife. When you miss someone, you even miss the way you got in trouble, like being awakened in the middle of the night because you forgot to wash the dishes. This might seem weird, but it was even the way the sun shined on a Sunday afternoon after church. I wanted to ask God these questions when he took his last breath. Did he know he was dying?? How did he feel about leaving us behind? Did he try and wait for us? Did he want to say goodbye? Did he want us up there as he took his last breath? I wish he could have left a video or voice note behind of his last moments. Maybe his last moments did not have to be sad. We could have shared a last laugh or joke or just seen him smile one more time. Or maybe God did not want us to see him take his last breath. Maybe when he left this earth, it was just him and God. Someone said they watched our dad take his last breath. I never believed it, and to this day, I am not sure why this person chose to do that. I wanted to give her the benefit of the doubt. Maybe she did see it, but if that were even true, why not just keep that moment to yourself, knowing we didn't get the chance even to say goodbye? Unfortunately, this person was known as an attention seeker, so I could not believe it. Why would God rob us of that moment and give it to you? It took my family and me years to forgive her. Yes, we were just that hurt by a simple comment. He left us on Wednesday at 1:52 p.m. The first couple of weeks were weird. It still felt like he was still in the hospital or on the world's longest business trip.

We did not go home for a few days, and if we did, it would only be to get a few things. The apartment was a little strange going back there. He was not there sitting in his computer chair or at the edge of the bed studying his word. We stayed at our grandmother's house for the next few days. This is where most of the funeral plans were made. I do wish my little brothers and I were involved with the planning. We could've given a song choice. We knew his favorite gospel songs. Or picked out who we wanted to sing. Or even some flower colors, but no one is honestly thinking straight during things like this. My mama and Emmanuel, along with my dad's brother, Uncle Luke, our great Uncle Melvin, and our dad's cousin Jackson, who was also a pastor of his own church, did all the planning. Ezekiel and I stood in the corner of the hallway so we could sneak and listen. We did not like anything that was suggested. The song choices were blah, the choir was blah, and some of the people listed to sing were blah. We preferred for the choir from our cousin Jackson's church to sing. I loved their choir, and so did my mom. The only thing that we smiled at was who was doing the funeral service. They wanted two nights, two services; my mother said no; she did not want to put us or herself through any more pain. She was at that point where she wanted it to be over with already. No one enjoys picking caskets and planning a funeral for their husband, anyone really.

It was the morning of the funeral, and all-black limos were pulling up to my grandmother's house. We were all dressed in blue with blue ribbons pinned to us. My mama suggested we should wear blue; it was his favorite color, and the ribbon was for cancer. I could feel the anxiety rising inside me. Even right now, rewriting this for you, I can feel that same anxiety. Even walking to the limos, even now, it is replaying in my head everything that happened while getting into the limos. Once we got to the church, my mama was quiet while the family was lining up. My mama asked me to walk next to her, but something happened to where my aunt ended up walking with her instead, which was probably best because we both could not be falling out and breaking down. Goin'up yonder! We marched into "Goin' Up Yonder." I don't even think my mama picked that song. I remember hearing it on the radio one Sunday night, and our dad told us how, growing up, he was afraid of that song as a kid. I mean, think about you're a kid, and you hear this lady with a big voice singing about goin' up yonder, and you're thinking to yourself, *where is yonder, and why is she going up there?* Although it was played nicely on the keyboard, it was still taunting. To tell you the truth, it took me a while to really listen to that song. As I have gotten older, I must say I do enjoy it, and it might be because I know what she is speaking about. I oddly catch myself humming it. It still gives me chills.

I didn't want to see him lying in that casket, but there he was sleeping. I wanted to touch him, but I just stood there. I didn't know what to do, really. He looked peaceful. I thought to myself, *do I fall out crying? Do I break down in tears? Do I jump in there with him?* I stood there for a second, put my head down, and took my seat in the front row next to Emmanuel and Ezekiel. No one on the earth wants to see their loved one in a casket, let alone their parent. That feeling and that image is something that sticks with you for a while. Even when you try to think of the good times, that picture of them lying there is in your head. His casket was light blue on the inside and dark blue on the outside, with a faint cross on top. It was beautiful. There was this huge portrait with his face on it, which was a blanket. The funeral home made it special for my mom. It was very nice and very life-like. His eyes were staring at you the whole service. My dad's cousin, Pastor Jackson Miller, did such a good job with everything.

Of course, some black folk can not have a funeral without foolishness. I mean, there were a few over-dramatic stunts and falls. So, there I was, sitting there in my seat, listening to the choir sing. Suddenly, I saw a young lady who used to go to my dad's church and who also had a disagreement with his views on the church in the past fall right smack dab in the middle of my brother Emmanuel's lap right after her A, B selection. I sat there and thought how inappropriate and unnecessary this was. It was completely over the top. I felt like she wanted to have a moment and make a scene. She wanted to be noticed. I wanted to whisper right in her ear and tell her to get her you-know-what up and stop her foolishness seriously.

Nobody helped her get up, not even her own husband. Everybody just looked at her. Emmanuel just sat there unfazed, waiting for her to get up. Toward the end of the service, it seemed like all the sadness fell at once. So I will set the tone for you: the choir breaks out with "Every Praise is to Our God," another song we had to get over. It took us a while to move on from it. I could still hear the cries and picture his casket rolling down the aisle.

My little brother Ezekiel wanted to see his face one last time. He asked for his casket to be reopened, and my cousin, Pastor Jackson, made sure it happened. He waved goodbye one last time for this lifetime. Of course, the entire church stopped. I don't think anyone's eyes were dry. I watched him break down in tears. I saw my dad's brother so upset. He sat through the whole service with his fist balled up. We all finally had a breakdown. I heard my mother, Priscilla, scream at the top of her lungs, "Please don't go," as they continued to carry him out of the church. It took me a while to get her scream out of my head. She suddenly started speaking in tongues, and the spirit hit her, and she fell out (Speaking in tongues: a heavenly language between you and God). All of my uncles and aunt ran to her aid. I believe the Holy Spirit came to comfort her. I just wanted an angel to come down from heaven and help. I wanted God to wake him up. Yes, even then, I was still hopeful for a miracle.

Chapter 5

THE HEAVENLY GATES WILL OPEN FOR HIM

*E*verything coordinated perfectly; even our limo driver said she had never been to a service like that. She had never been to a completely fully packed-out service to the point where there were no seats left. She said, "Wow, he was truly loved." My mama's family from a small town called Temple, Texas, said, "Wow, I cannot believe we just shut down one of the main major freeways in Houston." The procession line were the only cars on the freeway. My aunt said that was God bringing his child home.

Our dad was loved. He always went out of his way to help Everybody, no matter if it was his day off or if he had just come home from a full day and went back to help someone. Our time at the gravesite was short; my mama was ready to go, and of course, we all followed. Honestly, I did not want to finish the rest of the day, and neither did my siblings. We had family waiting for us back at our grandmother's house. It did not feel like we had just buried him. It felt like we just left him there alone, like we dropped him off somewhere.

When you were younger, did you ever think of losing your parents or grandparents? These people, in your eyes, are supposed to live forever. Did you ever think of the possibility of going through life without them? How empty or how lonely it would be without them? Like, did you ever think that day would come when you could not call them? Because after you lay them to rest and when the phone calls stop, this might be how you start thinking. Your mind might play tricks, or you might even have a dream or two about them, but make sure you remember the good times, not how they suffered. You will get angry a time or two, but do not let it consume you. Try to be happy like they would have wanted you to be. Make their favorite meal or watch their favorite shows. For us, it was "Dallas," "The Jeffersons," "Good Times," etc. Pray every day. Talk to God a lot and remember to cry to release your pain, and hey, it's okay to have a sad day. Do not let anyone tell you when to stop crying; this is your process. Do not hold on to that hurt or pain. Do not blame yourself. Just because you continue living does not mean you forgot about them. We needed to make sure we helped our mama the best way we could. We allowed her to go through her time. She never once broke in front of us. We were not going to let her stumble.

After everything was done, I graduated high school. Yes, we went through all this while still in school. All of our friends knew. Most of my classmates that I was close to knew. I do not know how, but we just went to school. I went to prom with my now husband, Andrew. Ezekiel and Elijah graduated a year behind me. It sucks that he missed it. It sucked that he would be missing out on his grandkids and future grandkids growing up, weddings, and other big accomplishments. We wanted to make him proud of us with every choice we made. It was silent most of the time in the apartment. I always had trouble sleeping since I was younger, but after he passed, it seemed like everyone had turned into a night owl. I would always ask him to come in and bless my room with holy oil. I always felt like somebody was walking into my room or looking over me while I slept. I would wake up and go to my mom's room. It would be three in the morning, and she would be up on the computer listening to gospel music. We all had to adjust; it just was not normal.

Trouble hit us hard, and we began to have problems, one of them being financial. I mean, . Remember, I did mention we were not rich, but we had everything we needed. So, we went from something to nothing. A few months and a year or so went by, and unfortunately, we began to have problems on top of problems. None of our family members knew how badly we were off. My mama never spoke about it with anyone, not even to this day, and it stayed like that for a while. Our dad had filled out his retirement paperwork before he passed away. This paperwork was put in place, so our mama could be financially okay for a long time. But it would be months before we would see anything. And when it finally came, it was like here and gone. The faster it came, the faster it left. We only had enough just to pay rent, and on top of that, the apartment we were staying in decided to go up on the rent after they found out my daddy passed.

We did not even have money for things like tissue paper. We just did not have the basic things you needed for a home. Are you thinking, how come we did not ask for help? Asking for help and feeling a burden are two different things. We just didn't want to be a burden. You could ask for help, but you wonder if people are going to talk about you behind your back. It makes you feel hopeless.

My best friend, someone I trusted, still to this day, would give me a little money here and there. She also worked at a pizza shop, and without even knowing if we had food, she brought us a box. She knew my family for years, and she always had extra to give. Her dad would buy pounds and pounds of stuff, so she always had extra. Her home was like a mini-Costco, so she knew it would not hurt her, and she was happy to help. And when we did get on our feet, we definitely returned the favor. Emmanuel would often help us out as much as he could, but my mama hated taking money from her son, knowing he had a family. She just was not built like that. She did not want to go to her sisters because they had mortgages and people to take care of as well. She just did not want to bother them. I would lie or give an excuse as to why I could not go hang out with some of my best friends. They knew we were having trouble, but only a few knew how deep. I could not eat out with them like they wanted me to or go bowling and do other fun things. I did not even know if I would be eating dinner that night. They would always be like, "Just come, and we will pay for you." If they only knew half of what was going on with my family and me, they did not even know they were feeding me for the day. I would feel guilty thinking that my mama and brothers were back at home hungry and I was wrong to be out enjoying myself.

Sometimes, we had to just stick it out. We did not have any room to complain. Sure, we could have broken our lease and moved in with a family member to save money. But who wants to do that and end up being a burden or overstaying your welcome? We just prayed and believed for better days to come. Sometimes, I could not afford my medication. We lost our insurance. Understanding the cost of insulin is unbelievably expensive, and it was tough. Nothing made me sadder than seeing my mama cry or looking worried because she could not help her family the way she needed to. Nobody knew the trouble we had or the conditions we were living in. It did not seem like things were letting up for us. One thing for certain was that we are not the type of family to ask for pity, and we didn't get it.

I thought about suicide once. I thought maybe if I were not around, my mom would have one less mouth to feed, and my mom could just focus on her and my brothers and no expensive meds to buy. I know it was a stupid thought, and thank God I did not act on it. For one, funerals are expensive, so I would have made our money problems worse, not better, and the pain I would have caused my family would have been selfish of me. Yes, I have asked God to forgive me. I know that talking like that was stupid, and some might call it a cop-out, but it just felt like we were in a hole, and every time we were close to digging out of it, it seemed like we just kept getting stuck.

I did not think I was doing enough to help her. It was just her by herself now. Of course, she had her family and us, but she lost her best friend and the love of her life. One day, a huge fight broke out between my brothers. I mean, we fought, but this was like a brawl, and I cried out to my mama repeatedly, asking her why he had to leave us like this. It felt like, for a while, we could not get it together. We started to fall apart, which is the opposite of what we should be doing. We were supposed to be helping our mama and sticking together. In my mind, it felt like when our dad left, a small piece of our mama left, too. All his things were still in our apartment; his favorite cologne never left the spot he placed them in. Walking into our mother's bathroom, sometimes it smelled like it had just been sprayed. His hats, clothes, and shoes were still hanging in the closet. His collection of Bibles and Sunday School lesson books sat on the edges of the computer table. The one thing we were worried about happening happened. There was an eviction notice left on the door. We were embarrassed. My mom tried her hardest to work with our leasing office, but it seemed nobody wanted to hear it.

Some of the people in our leasing office began to pick on us and refused to fix anything or change out the carpet we had for over ten years. Bank accounts were closing, and cell phones were being shut off. It was a domino effect. One year, for Christmas, when we did not think we were going to have Christmas dinner, we had to go to the food bank to get food. I know it was just food, and there are a lot of people that have absolutely nothing. We were blessed and grateful. It was just something we were not used to and something we did not want to get used to, and it was just not the food; it was the feeling of hopelessness. But my mama made it work with the food they gave. It was one of the best meals we had in a while.

What was still shaky was the relationship between my siblings and me. We were verbally attacking each other, sometimes physically. We pointed our emotions and frustration at each other. Sometimes, we would not even speak. It was weird because we were brothers and sisters. It should be easy to pick up the phone and call one another. We had disrespected each other in so many ways that the jokes and laughter between us did not exist for a while. We were breaking our mama's heart and really acting like fools with no sense.

I was venting to friends only to get talked about and having our business spread to other people like wildfire. I had my family's situation thrown up in my face by people who claimed to be my friends. I had people talk about my mama. They would call her stupid or lazy and even laugh at the fact that our daddy was no longer living and she was alone. The same people who sat at my table and were eating my mama's cooking and sat at my dad's funeral were now laughing and talking about my family and me while we were going through our tough times. I just wanted things to go back to normal. I wanted Jesus to send an angel down and help us. I was hoping things would get better and we would not have to go through this too much longer.

September 4th was my twenty-first birthday; it was my second year without our dad. My parents made our birthdays special for us. My mama would bake us a cake and cook our favorite meal. Around this time, things had gotten much better for us. I didn't do much that year. She made my favorite meal and some cupcakes. I know what you're thinking. It was my twenty-first, a milestone birthday. I just wasn't into it that year or any after that, really. Every birthday at midnight, we always thanked God for another year. We would run around singing "Happy Birthday," which we still do to this day. It was important we kept that with us. I don't think people understand how much of a blessing a birthday truly is or life itself. This year, I asked God for a special gift. I wanted to hear or dream of my dad saying happy birthday to me in his normal speaking voice before the cancer took over. I did not want to remember how his voice was when he left here. They say when you go to heaven, your body is made brand new, so I knew I would hear him clearly if I heard him at all.

One day, while sitting at the computer table in my mama's room, our home phone rang. My mama made sure all the bills were moved to her name. For a while, the phone would sometimes switch, meaning when someone called, it read his name instead of the person who was calling. It stopped for a long while. Although it had stopped for a while, the fact that on this day it rang and read his name, I knew it was my gift. My mama had the phone in her room. She picked it up and showed me. I was shocked, nervous, and a little scared. I knew what I had asked for. As a certain presence came over me, I hurried up and answered the phone. The background sounded like air, like someone was sitting next to an open window, and the wind was just blowing. I said hello, and all I was getting was the sound of air. After a few minutes, I did hang up, hoping I did not hang up too fast. It gave me goosebumps. When I explain it to people, I call it my phone call from heaven; even though I did not hear his voice, I knew it was him. I missed my dad a lot, but sometimes, I would feel guilty because I wouldn't cry every day. I knew he would want us to be happy and not just sit around crying, but the feeling of going on and enjoying life seemed unfair.

Like, should I be crying? Should I be walking around angry? I did not want my dad to think I did not miss him. But we would always pretend he was away on a business trip. It was like a comfort for me. For some reason, I would feel peaceful, then angry, then peaceful again, and then sometimes, I just did not understand why it had to be this way. I wanted him to be here with us. He was only forty-three. His best years weren't even here yet, but we understood that life with Jesus is eternal.

As time went on, that empty feeling without him got better. My mama told us it was not easy, but because of God, she made it. It was God who kept her sane and focused, reminding her that she had kids and a family that loved her.

She did not stay locked up in her room; she had times when she needed to be alone, but she never gave up. People did not think she would make it, but she did for us and herself. She did not ask us for anything. She begged us to take care of ourselves. She never hit us with the, "I gave you life. I provide for you." She never once made it feel like we owed her. And honestly, she never had to ask us for anything we wanted to do it. We wanted to help. She was our mother.

Once my health got a little bit better, I got a part-time job down the street from our home. A department store was hiring for holiday help, and I took it. Even though it was temporary, I thanked God that I got it, and I was lucky it was within walking distance. It was my first job, and it was not too bad.

I made fifteen an hour, which back then was a lot of money. This was before we started receiving our dad's checks consistently. I loved working and helping the household and doing what I could. We ate hot dogs for a long time. I mean every day. I could not stand to eat or see another hot dog. We ate hot dogs and 99-cent hamburgers so much back then. The sausage could range anywhere between $0.99 to $1.98. The hot dog chili was $1.75, two bags of fries were at least $2.98, and it was $2.00 for two liters of regular soda for the boys and diet for my mom and me, which back then was a luxury for us.

We still needed help here and there, but things were getting better little by little, and we were finally able to manage things. I enjoyed helping my mama out. I felt like her partner. I felt like an adult, like a real adult. It felt good to take some worries off her hands. I knew people were talking about us at their dinner table, waiting for everything to fall apart. I knew they wanted us to struggle and keep hitting each other upside the head, and at one point, we proved them right. For a long time, it seemed like we could not do anything, and all we could do was struggle and fight. We never once claimed to be perfect. But this wasn't us; we knew God had His hands on us.

Chapter 6

AFTER YOU
WENT HOME

Something else we needed to figure out was going back to church. It was something that we did every Sunday since the day we were born. And it was now a major question of whether we wanted to go back or not. We knew just waking up and getting ready for church was going to be different from this point on. It was going to be hard to walk into the church without him. We'd done it before, but this time, his seat was forever empty. I'm not saying it was not hard for anyone else. It was the fact that our daddy, our pastor, the man we had seen preaching and praying for other people all these years, was no longer here. It was an empty feeling at home and an empty feeling at church. I know it was church, but it did hit differently going there and not seeing him sitting in his chair with his Bible in his lap and a highlighter in his hand while busting out in a song. My mama, of course, did not force us to go back. She thought it was too soon, which was true. We jumped right back in; it was too soon. Speaking for myself, I found it easy just to say no to going back to church right away. It was strange to go and even more strange to sit at home.

I do not think right away we were wondering who would be taking his place as pastor at the church. It was clear we still needed time to process things and how things were about to change, mostly with leadership. Who was going to lead us? Who would pray for the deaf lady who would come in off the street mid-service to ask for prayer? We, speaking as his children, wanted to make sure our daddy's legacy was remembered in every way possible. Not to upstage anyone or put anyone on a pedestal; we weren't trying to make him perfect. But he was important to us. It wasn't like anybody else was going to acknowledge our daddy and the impact he had on people and how he was a godly man inside and out. This is for his grandkids and future grandkids. They needed to know their grandfather could preach the house down. He taught us that we have to praise God no matter what the situation, never give up, and not walk out on God. Even in my daddy's last days, he praised God. He always kept the faith.

My brothers and I picked out a nice picture of him and a nice cherry wood picture frame for it. We used our dad's old desk name tag that he used for work. It was gold, so it went perfectly. To get the name tag to stick, we had to use double-stick duct tape so it would stay. Of course, it was not professionally done, but that is all we had. To us, it felt like no one at the church wanted to honor him, not worship, but honor him. We just wanted him to be remembered a little bit better. This is why we felt this way. Even after being told by a different pastor how certain things needed to be done after a leader passes away, somehow, these things just never got done, and yes, we felt sad about it. He never asked for anything and never asked to be celebrated. He was one of those preachers who didn't have to sit in the pulpit. He was fine with just sometimes sitting in the back. But we felt the most you could do now that he was gone was to follow simple instructions on honoring him as the former leader of the church.

We wondered what was next. He never announced nor left any handwritten letter behind on who he preferred to take his place. However, we did believe he had someone in mind who was already showing up to preach on Sundays even before he passed away.

One Sunday, my mama came to church with us. It had been years since my mother had been there. This Sunday was set aside for a special voting that was going to take place between some of the seasoned members. This vote was to determine who would be the next pastor. It had not been six months since he had been gone, but you could tell things were getting pushed aside. Everything seemed so rushed, like it was happening overnight. In our eyes, no one could take his spot in church. But honestly, it was not about our personal feelings. It was about the saints and souls that needed to be saved and the unsaved trying to get there. Somehow, this so-called vote never happened, at least not with us. It turned into a shocking, already prepared, ready-to-go announcement. Jaws dropped, and faces hit the floor. It was announced that our Uncle Melvin was now our pastor. You are thinking this is good. He is your uncle, keeping it in the family.

The entire church was stuck and shaken, except the ones that secretly knew already. My mama was furious and angry. Her frustration came from a much deeper place. She was told one thing and persuaded to come. After so many phone calls, she finally decided to show up, and something else took place. One thing about my mama is that she hates being lied on and lied to, and she cannot stand when people are being fake with her. You know that look you give someone when you are the last one in the room to find out something? That was the look everyone had. She was asked to come there and state her opinion to offer a helping hand. She was the widow of our late pastor. Growing up and attending other churches, I always loved how much appreciation and respect they had for their first lady. My mama never really got that. You could cut the tension with a knife. My great aunt was shocked as well because she was begged to come, also. She tried to calm my mother down as they both were upset, but at this point, emotions began to grow and take over. The announcement was planned way before, weeks before, maybe even months before.

We knew a little bit of how behind-the-scenes church business went. We knew there were different steps to go through before even reaching this pastoral status. There were already little rumors beginning to spread; it was already said this would happen. The only wrong thing was the time, date, and place. But everything else was right. I grabbed the car keys from my brother and quickly tried to get my mama out of there. He did try to stop and explain himself to my mama. He told her it had to be done this way. The church could not be taken away. But the damage was done. My mama had already felt tricked and played. The thought of someone other than my daddy standing in that pulpit on Sunday preaching or sitting in his chair. We, as his kids, were just not ready for someone new, but we weren't against someone coming in preaching God's word. This was God's house, and if they were coming in preaching God's word, then who are we to say anything? His taking his place wasn't the issue; it was the way everything went down. Every single part of the situation was sneaky.

It was funny how quickly the pastor situation came about, but when it came to our dad being remembered in the right way, instead, it was very lackluster. There was no wreath outside the door showing a remembrance of a pastor who had just passed. His chair where he sat was not even draped; it seemed like no one cared.

We did not get a chance to pick who we wanted to be head leadership. We did not get a chance to be heard. We had no say so, but the deed was done. We watched our father sit up under someone for a while. We saw him work at it, but it seemed like it was just handed to my uncle. We wondered who groomed him and who helped him. We had a lot of questions but no answers. Do not get me wrong, I am not being a hater or being disrespectful to a man of God. He was still our uncle, and we loved him truly, but things just did not seem right. We figured if you were already given this position, why make a big uproar and claim it was a vote when it really was you just telling us something that you did behind our backs?

We didn't love him any less, but I mean, of course, we were very hurt. This cut us deeper than we thought. Trying to separate the two titles of pastor and uncle, believe it or not, they are different people. We respected and loved him as our uncle. But on the pastoral level, it was not clicking with us. We tried, but we could not. It had a lot to do with the way he got it; it was questionable to us. The kicker was he started saying things like our daddy was going to pick him and our daddy wanted him to be the leader, which was not true at all. Speaking for myself, watching him sit in his chair and watching certain changes begin didn't seem fair to me. It did not seem right. I knew I should not be focused on those things while in church. I should have been focused on Jesus and the Word, but it was hard to shake off my feelings about the situation.

One Sunday in church, I let my mind wander off. I honestly thought I heard my daddy's voice. I thought I saw him walking across the church, fully dressed in one of his blue suits. Only to realize, of course, that I was just staring into space. With a tear running down my face, I got up and went to the restroom. I imagined what I desperately wanted to see.

We gave it our all. We did our best. We did not want to stop going to the church we grew up in. We had memories there. We were going with a broken spirit, coming home empty and more broken. At one point, it did start to feel like just tradition. But we were far more than willing to give our Uncle Melvin a chance. We set aside our feelings and decided to really give it a go, okay. But we had to understand we were just going to church to go. Our souls were still hungry. We eventually fell back and stopped going. We grew a little distant. The relationship between niece, nephew, and uncle was changed completely. Leaving was not what we wanted to do but what we needed. We did not want to hurt his feelings, but at the end of the day, we needed to be filled with the word of God. We just felt like we didn't get that. On top of that, some unfair things were going on behind the scenes.

It was the second church anniversary under new leadership, and my brother and his fiancé went to the church to help set up some decorations and clean the church. You know, give the church a fancy look and make it look sparkly and shiny. Of course, me being me, I thought, *oh wow, no one ever went out of their way to do this for my dad*. But suddenly, things that I would have liked the church to do for him were being done. Someone could have lightened his load a little. Most people do not know this, but pastors go through a lot. Sometimes, they get sick. Sometimes, they do not feel their best emotionally. They are pastors, not bulletproof vests. They go through trials like everybody else.

Someone already wanted to erase and replace him fully. They wanted to take his picture down, not just his picture but also our great uncle, who was the founder. They said it would give the church a fresh look. But the decorations were not even permanent, and on top of that, it was the church anniversary. If anything, those should be kept up there. She insisted on them being gone. We dealt with her before, and for some reason, every encounter with her was the same - rude. I guess she did not want those pictures to outshine his big moment as the new pastor.

Why do you want to remove history, especially one of them being the person who started the church? It was a picture that we, as the grieving family, took the time to put up because no one else was going to do it.

No one was going to remove that picture, no one. No one could tell us how or when to let go; no matter how long it had been, we were not going to let go. Someone had the nerve to tell my mother she had six months to grieve. We could not believe someone actually said that to her. I heard it with my own two ears. I thought to myself, *really, was this a joke? She lost her best friend. She had known this man since high school. There is no time limit on grief.*

We watched him suffer. Nobody was at home with us, watching his weight fall off and him coughing up blood every day, having to go to school with a smile on our faces, thinking and wondering if our dad was going to be alive when we got home from school. So, to say that was just not right. Was it a joke? Were they just being funny, like in a dark humor kind of way? You would think that's the last straw, huh, and we would finally leave? Well, we did for a little while.

A few months went by, and we decided to give it another try, so we just popped up unexpectedly, but we also chose this Sunday to sit down and talk with our uncle. After the service, we waited until everyone was gone and began to tell our truth finally. But it just seemed like he did not get it. My mama agreed that there was nothing wrong with going to him respectfully and letting him know what he did was wrong while letting him know we still loved him and were still his family. We had questions. We felt like he played us. We felt like he was allowing certain people from other churches to come in and mistreat us and treat us like we did not exist. This talk would sadly not be our first go-round. Sadly, it went nowhere. We tried and tried and tried, but for me, it was the last straw. Our dad always taught us to respect the men of God, men that God has called to do His work. In other words, do not put your mouth on anyone God has chosen to relay His message. But there was this evangelist from another church who, in my opinion, had always had a rude and mean way of thinking of my brothers and me. She came to the church and decided to do an altar call. Now, my daddy and mama both told us not to let everybody lay hands on us and to have discernment. If I know you don't like me, then why would I allow you to pray for me? I have no idea where your heart is. As we were up there, she began to prophesy over us, but the things she said about Elijah were so off; something about it didn't seem right.

If you know my little brother, he's a big nerd in a good way, meaning his way of a good time is beating one of his many games and reading one of his many books. He spends his Saturdays watching Marvel movies with my other little brother Elijah and going to different bookstores. But the things she was saying made it seem like he was out here running through these streets. She told him he was running with the wrong crowd and this crowd was going to get him in so much trouble.

Everything she was saying sounded exactly like someone else. I knew she was speaking to the wrong person. I picked my head up and thought, *is anybody listening to this? Was anyone hearing what I was hearing?* I just respectfully wanted to tell her to stop. I saw the look on our uncle's face; it was a look of disbelief like he knew what she was saying was wrong, but he did not say anything. Days went by after that, and we finally heard from him. He apologized for allowing her to do that, and he said he should've stopped her. He said he knew that wasn't his nephew's character, not even close to it. Once again, we were left feeling mistreated.

Why not stop her right there? Why come and apologize in secret? Even after that, we gave it another chance.

Once again, I decided to join my brothers one Sunday. Everything was going good. When you read this part of the story, keep in mind Elijah has autism; he does not like large crowds, he keeps his head down most of the time in public, and he doesn't like loud noises, but church was an exception. But at this time, he was going through a phase where he didn't want anyone saying his name. He didn't even want us saying it at home. During praise and worship service, his name was said over the microphone. They were just pointing out people and saying how glad they were to see everyone. I knew he had become annoyed. I took him outside before anything could happen, and he told me he was calm and okay. While getting up to go to the restroom, our uncle was walking and speaking over the microphone. He tried to make his way to him and hug him. In my head, when I saw him, I said, *oh Lord, this is not going to end well, and this is going to set him off*. He was still upset with our uncle. Imagine the person you're upset with coming to hug you. He was aware that changes were being made and that his daddy's legacy was being erased. He didn't allow his condition to hold him back. He did and said exactly how he felt. He knew his feelings should be valued.

He knew what was right and what was wrong. He knew hurt and pain. He may understand this world differently from everyone else, but he knew what was going on. My uncle tried to pray for him. Just because someone refuses prayer from you doesn't always mean they have the devil in them. My brother didn't want it, and my Uncle Melvin just pressed and pushed the issue until Ezekiel just blew up. He screamed through the whole church, yelling, "Don't touch me. Just don't touch me." He pushed him away. He almost picked up a chair to throw. My other brothers immediately got up, grabbed him, and proceeded to try and get him out of the church. Ezekiel was very much built like a linebacker. So, trying to get him to settle down was a task. I yelled repeatedly, "Stop," as my uncle was still trying to come toward him, I said, "Stop, just leave him alone. Get away from him." I looked over and noticed one of the ladies from the church holding my two nieces tight next to her, pretending to calm them down, and they weren't even crying. My nieces and nephews knew of their uncle's condition. She actually made them cry, trying to make their uncle seem like a monster. They tried to make it seem like he had a devil inside of him. It was pure chaos that could've been avoided. My brother begged for them to stop, but they didn't stop. My aunt held on to herself in fear, like he was going to attack her. It was awful. It was terrible. Nothing, absolutely nothing, was the same after. He cried, and he was hurt and embarrassed. He looked at himself as if there was something wrong with him, and there wasn't.

Chapter 7

STANDING IN THE NEED OF PRAYER

*A*t this point, it was clear that we should just stop trying to make something happen that wasn't going to happen. If it was not clear to us, then it is for sure clear now. That was a wrap. We did not need to get hit with any more bricks. I think what happened to our brother, amongst other things that were happening, may have finally opened our eyes. People thought that we left because we were jealous of the new things being done around the church. We weren't jealous that he was pastor; we were fed up with the mistreatment and the foolishness of everything. We weren't searching for a spotlight. Sure, I wish while my dad was still alive, he would have gotten more help, but why continue to allow ourselves to be treated this way? And on top of that, we couldn't support a lie.

We had to write a letter, which was a more respectable way to leave. My brothers and I agreed it would always be our church home, and he would always be our uncle, but that was it. Little did we know Elijah had already had one prepared. He had been working on it for a while. He had put how he felt into words and sent it off. All he needed was an envelope and a stamp. It was better this way. Just the thought of having another conversation that would not go anywhere was draining. Talking about what ifs and a bunch of I did not know. It was a little sad that you couldn't just sit and talk to someone without them telling you it is the devil or not to let the devil use you instead of just admitting your faults.

One Saturday, we drove by the church and put it in the mailbox. After that, we let it be. To this day, we are not sure if he read it.

I mean, he never brought it up. We used to only do pop-ups when we knew the service was getting ready to end. My mama would ask us, "Why do ya'll keep doing this to yourselves?" She asked us a very valuable question, "Are you getting anything out of it? Because if you're not, you need to go somewhere where you are being fed." My mother reminded us that the devil knew the Bible, too. Don't think you're ungodly because you don't attend church and you have the devil in you if you choose to go to a different church where you are being fed the word of God and remember God is much bigger than that building because if that church was no longer standing does that mean God is gone? No, of course not. There were just certain things happening that I knew my daddy wouldn't allow to happen in the house of God. We wanted and needed to be in church; that's what we grew up doing. It was in us. We couldn't run from it even if we tried, and trust me, I have tried. It was time for something new, something fresh but still familiar. We decided to go to another family church. My brothers and I started going every now and then. We knew we would be getting nothing but the word of God. And as a plus, it was Holy Ghost-filled. It felt like home, like an old-school church. I had a moment where I just needed to step back and reflect on things, but once I got back into it, it felt so good getting back into church. There's nothing like spending a Sunday afternoon in God's house. Of course, some people found out we were going there, and he was a little hurt and upset and, of course, blamed it on the devil.

But it was not the devil, and it had nothing to do with anyone else's feelings. We weren't thinking about backstabbing anyone. We just wanted to go to church and get fed the word of God. We were willing and wanted to be there. How many young adults do you know That's running to God? I mean, it's just a handful of us in my generation. But once again, he made it about hurt and betrayal. We wrote, and we had talks, but no one understood what we were going through. We did not know if he wanted us to stay just to support him. We accepted him as an uncle. That wasn't going to change, but it felt like we were lied to and used as an agenda. My mother was hurt. She had many sleepless nights. It seemed like nobody acknowledged our pain and what we were going through, and every time we tried to explain what we were going through, we were called jealous or trying to stop someone's blessings.

They tried to make us feel like we were wrong for not supporting him and not staying there and helping him. They said it was disrespectful and jealous and that our blood was on their hands, telling us that our daddy would have wanted us to stay and that he would be disappointed in us. Family or not, he would've wanted us to go where the spirit was moving and where we were getting fed. It's about accepting Christ as your Savior and your own personal relationship with Jesus. In a way, your pastor is responsible for your soul as well. And, of course, we knew that. As a pastor, it's their job to help lead you down the right path. He is the shepherd. You are their flock, and when it's all said and done, in the end, heaven awaits you, of course.

It's kind of like saying, "You can lead a horse to water, but you can't make him drink." Like I have heard all my life, "It is either holiness or hell. The choice is yours." God gives us free will to serve him or not. Go somewhere that the word is being taught and where the Holy Ghost is welcomed. Don't go somewhere because of status. You see, I prefer to go somewhere where the pastor knows my name, not my seat number. But if God is in the building, then you're in the right building. And please, please use your discernment. We couldn't stay in an empty place.

You might be reading this thinking we're still mad and angry or even bitter, or you might be saying *it's not that bad ya'll could have stayed there and built that church up*. I think too much was already done. There were people there who weren't even members constantly trying to make us feel less than and trying to make us seem like we were basically haters. Sure, we could have tried to stay. It took a while. I mean, of course, when someone close to you hurts you, it's going to burn a little. Forgiveness is sometimes easy. But forgetting is difficult. I didn't write this to hurt anyone or disrespect him. I have forgiven him. I let go of the hurt that happened. Sometimes, you must for yourself and because God wants you to. We must forgive, especially the body of Christ.

He was still our uncle, but who was going to tell our story? There were many things said and done in front and behind our backs. We love him. I remember one Sunday, Ezekiel and I went for a visit, and we were asked to come for something special. We came back home, changed clothes, and went. It was said that there was going to be a tribute to our daddy, so we said, of course, we should represent. I was asked if one of us would come and speak about our daddy and how he impacted people, so I wrote a nice, lengthy speech. I was ready, but it never happened. I never got a chance to say anything. If you tell me to write something nice and heartfelt, I am going to do it. I was more hurt than upset.

On top of that, the tribute that did happen was just two incorrect half-written paragraphs. Look, I am not saying my daddy is supposed to be praised, and by no means do I want to sound like a spoiled preacher's kid, but our daddy deserved something. I know his heavenly reward was waiting for him, but what about the earthly one?

It felt like we got hit with bricks. I mean a ton of bricks. It felt like we were just there for a show. It felt like, *let's just throw it together and ask them to come.* I remember being pregnant with my firstborn, and some of my daddy's old church preacher friends were there. And one of the pastors' wives gave me a look of disgust, and it was hurtful. I tried to speak to them, and they looked at me like I was dust. I wonder if they would have done that with my daddy still alive. I felt like I was being judged by certain people who started saying things about my family that were wrong. My older brother's business was shared with people who had no business in his business, if you know what. I mean, I was pregnant. I did not murder anyone. But yes, if you are wondering, I have let go of that hurt, too, and forgiven and moved on. Plus, babies are blessings, and God allowed me to carry my baby, so why should I be ashamed? Do not put your faith in people. You put your faith in God. People may promise you the world from here to the moon and then end up letting you down. Do not let people determine how you operate with God because of human error. Remember, God is God, and He can't lie. His word does not change, and do not let people run you out of church. You keep going, and when you pray for yourself, remember to keep praying for them.

So now we're at the end of the book. I started writing this book in the year 2016. So what's changed? Well, we still attend our other family church. Our relationship with our uncle is pretty much the same, honestly. But he does try and call at least one of the four of us. However, when we think about the past and what happened, we get more sad than angry, and we can actually laugh about most of the stuff that happened. We miss our dad every single day because every day something reminds us of him, especially on Sundays. It still hurts, but with time, things did get better. Sometimes, it's the way the sun shines on a Sunday afternoon. It always brings me back to when I was a little girl and walking with my Bible under my arm, going to my front door, and smelling my mama's cooking as soon as we came through the door or when my older brother Emmanuel would hit the keys on the organ without even reading a note. On Sunday evenings, the local radio stations at a specific time would play this instrument like clockwork. It would bring so much joy to my heart. I still smile when I hear it because it reminds me of our daddy. I always wondered if he was proud of us.

I also miss the old church days. Now, I'm in my late 20s, but where I grew up, church was beating a tambourine senseless while someone was singing. "Help me, help me, Lord, I need your help, help me, help me, Lord," and clapping until your hands were red and itchy, watching people catch the Holy Ghost running around the church because they couldn't help it. You just walked into a praise break, and now the preacher can't even preach because the spirit of God came in, and it's impossible. What happened to the old school preachers who would get on their knees and pray in the pulpit before they preached, and the mothers of the church who would carry purses full of safety pins and different color peppermint and would bring you a prayer cloth because your dress was a little too short? Even though it scared you, they were preaching the truth. Those are the Sunday services I'm talking about, not the big productions that they do today. That's the church we needed. That's the church we had.

So even though we left our church home to go to our secondary church home, we felt like time wasn't lost. We felt we were coming back to a home filled with what we needed. You shouldn't leave church how you came, meaning if you are sad, broken, angry, or lost, you should go home happy, joyful, and whole. Church is a place of refuge where you can find your hope in God again. It's a place of healing. Do not let people tell you there's something wrong with you because you love God and love going to church. Everybody has a story. This does not make us extra special because I chose to tell our story of a middle-class family going through tragedies we overcame. You could not tell me in a million years that I would see our daddy's name carved into a headstone. As unfair as it was, we watched him do everything right. He did what God called him to do. His mission was complete, and if I want to see him, I have to live right as well. You have to walk the walk and talk the talk and be Christ-like and forgive and let go of the things that are keeping you in the spirit of delay.

It was really our faith that kept us. We lost two uncles in the same year and our grandmother at the beginning of the following year. Most of my cousins and my aunts were in the room when she took her last breath. My mama's older sister was actually praying. As we stood there, the monitors went silent. My mama sadly buried her on her birthday. My older brother and his fiancé, Mia, had sadly lost their daughter. We've been down and broke, talked about, and mistreated. I had been sick in the hospital bed due to a lack of insulin, and the doctor looked me in the face and said I should've died. We have walked in the rain and heat to make sure we had food because transportation was up and down. We've had to live with mold, mildew, mice, and roaches and had people laugh at us.

So yeah, we have been through some dark moments. We have questioned our faith and asked God why. But God was still there through it all. He didn't leave us, and He's still here with us, allowing us to move forward. Just because life went on didn't mean we were forgetting him. I thank God for waking us up every morning. I thank God for bringing us out of those dark times. I thank God for giving us everything we need and more.

Tragedies can bring you close or tear you apart, and even though it got rough for a minute, we did not stay there. I'm not a preacher or anything, but I do not need to be to know that God kept us;

even if we didn't want to be kept, we are still standing because of God. The point of this story is to show you life is hard, even for a preacher's family. We were not invincible to storms coming our way. We knew God loved us. He wasn't punishing us. He did not want to hurt us; we had to learn to lean on Him and trust Him. Just because you go through a storm doesn't mean God loves you less. During a storm, He wants to hear from you the most. Please don't give up on God. Nobody is too far gone for God to reach out and grab them. Keep praying and keep the faith. It can't rain forever. The sun has to shine again.

So, like my daddy used to say, be blessed, and may heaven smile upon you.

THIS IS JANUARY CAME.